Side Hustle

Blueprint

How to Make an Extra $1000 Per
Month Writing eBooks!
(without leaving your day job!)

READ THIS FIRST

I've found that readers get the most success with this book when they check things off as they go along as well as follow a plan...

Just to say thanks for downloading my book, I'd love to give you access to the Side Hustle Blueprint Action Guide for 100% FREE!

Download Now:
www.outsourcedfreelancingsuccess.com/side-hustle-blueprint-guide

1. Welcome

An Introduction

~ ~ ~

*Before we get started, this guide is designed to be read AFTER the first book in this series, **Side Hustle Blueprint: How to make an extra $1000 in 30 days without leaving your day job**.*
If you haven't read that yet, you can pick it up here: www.outsourcedfreelancingsuccess.com/ SideHustleBlueprint - it provides the foundation you need to get things going from a Side Hustle perspective. This includes how to find clients, how to receive payments and how to set up your side hustle business the RIGHT way!

~ ~ ~

Congratulations. You've decided that to make your side hustle work for you, you're going to use the skills you have as a writer and walk the path as an book writer. More specifically, you're going to write ebooks or ghostwrite them.

You know the ones I'm talking about, ebooks like this one you're reading right now, which you can find on Kindle, Kobo, iBooks, Barnes and Nobles, etc, etc.

But. You're not sure where to start. Writing a book is not

something you've done before nor is it something you thought you'd ever do.

You want to do things right. You want to make some money but you also don't wanna end up with egg on your face, publishing (or writing) books that no-one wants to read.

I understand.

Picture this:

You've decided to write an ebook and publish it on Amazon. You've heard so many people are doing it and you figure why not? You set aside the weekend to write your ebook. You do this in MS Word and end up knocking out 20,000 words over the weekend! You're very proud of yourself...

You hand the ebook to an editor, who sends you back a document that has so much red 'track changes' that you can't even see what you wrote originally... you decide it's just too hard and go back to your 'normal' life.

Does this scenario sound at all familiar?

Or maybe, this is more like you:

You've been asked by a friend of a friend to ghostwrite an ebook for them. They agree to pay you $500 to write a

20,000 word non-fiction book. You're super excited, you can't believe that someone is willing to pay you to write!

You set aside the weekend to do it. You set up the book in MS Word, run it through a couple of spell checks and have your husband read it over. You email it off to the client Monday morning... a week goes by and nada. No emails, no response via phone either. All your hard work has walked out the door.

If these scenarios sound at all familiar to you (or not at all), then YOU know that writing ebooks, whether for yourself or someone else, requires a bit more planning and forethought than initially appears. Failure to get yourself set up the right way results in the above outcomes. Both of which are hard to come back from.

No matter what your situation is, I'm here to tell you that once you learn the process the right way, making money from writing ebooks is a solid side hustle income.

In the past three or so months (September to November) I've made over $5,000 USD in book sales! That's a nice little side hustle and one I'm sure you'd like to get your hands on as well.

Side Hustle Blueprint: How to Make an Extra $1000 per Month as an eBook Writer was written to help you achieve a better lifestyle, by providing you with a blueprint that shows you how you can make money as a book writer. And who knows, if you like this as much as I think you will, this could become your full-time side hustle!

This book is delivered in a succinct and easy-to-read manner, with action steps and plans to get you up and running with the least amount of fuss.

As a previous full-time employee who developed a side income without leaving my job, I mastered the art of creating income through my 'side hustles.'

Since I've been working full-time as a freelance writer, I've always wanted to write ebooks. I've spent the last 12 months researching and learning the inside secrets to be a successful self-published author.

I've spent over $5,000 in courses to learn all these secrets and now I want to share them with you. I know that you're time poor and probably don't want to spend that sort of money, so that's why I wrote this book - to provide YOU with the information you need to start your own book writing side hustle today.

And guess what, you don't need to leave your day job (unless you want too!) to be successful.

Although this book is designed to help you make some extra moola and increase your side hustling book writing skill set, to achieve these outcomes they need effort on your part. I'm doing my bit to get your started but you still need to do the hard work.

If you don't follow what's outlined in this book, nothing will change. It's that simple.

The steps outlined in this book provide you with a basis to get started and can be implemented and actioned by anyone, anywhere, no matter what type of job the person has.

Whether you're stuck working in an office, working from home, juggling new start-ups, or chasing the kids around the house, writing ebooks on the side is achievable, particularly if you focus on non-fiction books to begin with.

This book is split into the steps you need to take to set up your ebook writing side hustle.

You'll learn:

- The two types of book writing side hustle gigs you can use to make extra moola in the shortest amount of time
- How to write a book in 4 weeks — because if you wanna make money, you gotta be quick!
- How to edit the right way - without throwing yourself under the bus
- How to ensure your book sells!
- Best practices when ghostwriting books for clients

In the words of Richard Branson, *"The best way of learning about anything is by doing."*

Side Hustle Blueprint: How to Make an Extra $1000 per Month as an eBook Writer provides you with all the information you need to get started. You WILL make an extra $1000 per month in 30 days or less if you follow these steps.

Who knows, you might enjoy your book writing side hustle so much that you decide to make it your full-time gig, kicking that job of yours to the curb!

But, before you jump straight in, I'd like to share something with you that you should keep in the back of your mind while reading the book.

By following this one piece of advice, you put yourself in the top 10% of successful authors (think Stephen King, Elizabeth Gilbert etc!).

Failure to follow this one idea leads to unhealthy writing habits and wild expectations, rather than selling ebooks and making more good, consistent income.

Are you ready for it? Here it is...

Learn, Do, Repeat.

If you want to be successful at anything in life, you have to take ACTION.

Successful authors excel over unsuccessful authors because they understand the art of learning, doing and then repeating. They absorb and apply this learning quickly.

Authors who show up every day, write regardless of whether they feel like it or not are the ones that continue to be successful. Writing and self publishing ebooks provides an avenue that is far more accessible than it ever was before.

These successful authors learn more quickly and implement what works immediately.

How many times have you thought to yourself, "I WISH I earned more. I WISH I had another way of making extra money without having to risk my job," only to stop there and never take any further steps to do something about it?

Don't be the person that wishes and moans about wanting to earn more income or write a book, but never has the time. Don't be the person that sits and wishes they were making extra income, but does nothing to get that started.

Be the kind of person that other people look to for guidance; set an example.

Be the person that other people see and say, "I don't know

how they can afford to eat out all the time AND write amazing ebooks!"

Be the kind of person who implements what is learned and who takes action quickly.

The ideas presented in this book are proven to create what I feel are life-changing results. All you have to do to access the things you want and need financially is to keep reading and take action when told to. It's that simple.

Take control of your finances right now. Make them work for you, and create a lifestyle you love without all the extra stress of struggling to pay bills or worrying that your writing is not good enough to make money from.

On the next few pages, you're going to learn how exactly to use this guide. Then it's straight to the heart of it— Section 1 where we'll look at how you can get started writing books that make you moola. Turn the page to get started!

2. How This Guide Works

How to Use This Book to Your Advantage

LET'S GET something straight. Writing books is easy. Writing good books and making money from these books is where the difficulty lies.

This book will give you the exact steps I took to make some extra income from ebook writing - my very own side hustle. And while I am a full-time freelance writer, I have clients as well. So my time is not spent just writing books. In effect, this book writing business is my side hustle to my 'normal' freelancing work!

The best way to make this guide work for you is to follow the steps in the order they appear. Jumping ahead means you'll skip out on learning key points. As I mentioned, the book is split into two distinct sections:

1. You as an eBook Writer
2. You as a Ghostwriter of eBooks

If you feel that you already know something, I'd still

caution you about jumping ahead. But in the end, you know you, so I'll leave it up to you to make those decisions.

There is much to learn in the world of book writing, so make sure you pay close attention and take notes! By writing things down, you ensure that these are committed to your memory quicker than if you were typing them into your iPad or smartphone.

Before we get started, let's address the questions you're likely to have at this point. It's best to get these out of the way, so you can start with a clear head and no niggling voices trying to tell you otherwise!

Frequently Asked Questions About Starting an eBook Writing Side Hustle

Q: Do I need to know how to write properly?

A: I guess it depends on what you define as 'properly.' My own style of writing is conversational and direct, and this does really well in non-fiction books. Conversational writing is literally writing how you'd talk. So if you can do that, you're all set.

If you're new to writing, the more you write, the better you'll become. But in short, your editor will tidy up any grammar or spelling issues anyway!

Q: I've heard horror stories when it comes to ghostwriting books for others - how 'safe' is it to do this?

A: I'll go into more details about this in Section 2, but ghostwriting can be a really lucrative way to make money, provided you set your business up the right way. If you haven't already, go and pick up the first book "*Side Hustle Blueprint*" to learn how you should set up your business correctly.

Q: *How many hours do I need to set aside to make an extra $1000 per month?*

A: This is quite a subjective question and relies on your ability to write a book quickly or find clients to ghostwrite for.

You also need to be able to do the work that you're going to get paid to do. I spend 10+ hours on my book writing side hustle per week, while maintaining all my clients and other income streams as well.

I start work early and finish work around 4pm most days. This gives me a good couple of hours to work on my side hustle before my husband comes home. You decide how much time you can set aside for your side hustle and work from there.

In general, 5 hours or more per week is enough time to write an ebook, whether for yourself or ghostwriting, and to hit the $1000 per month mark.

Q: Will I need to spend any money to get started on my ebook writing side hustle?

A: Not at all, although I will make some recommendations to make your life easier along the way. You can be an ebook writer without spending a dime, if you're prepared to wear a few hats, i.e., editor, cover designer, formatter etc. The recommendations I do make are not costly - I love to bootstrap as much as possible!

If you have any further questions or feel that I haven't answered them in the book, please send an email to lise@outsourcedfreelancingsuccess.com. I respond to all emails within 24 hours.

Now that we've cleared up any misgivings you might have, let's get started.

In the next chapter, we're going to focus on Section 1 - Step 1 in this process. You're going to learn how to find ideas to turn into successful ebooks and then how to write a book in 4 quick weeks! Turn the page to learn more.

3. Step 1 - Research Ideas

Validate Your Idea

THIS STEP in the process is the most important one. If you don't get this step write (right!), no matter how good a writer you are, if there's no market, i.e., no-one wanting to buy your book, then you'll definitely not make any money.

There are a number of steps you need to take to ensure your idea is a good one, so follow the steps below and get your book idea validated.

If you don't have any ideas around what you want to write, check out my video on how to pick a niche on the Resources Page (you'll find the link to access the page in *Chapter 12*).

Step 1 - Validate your idea on Amazon

This is where you can quickly see whether the topic you've chosen is a good idea. If you didn't watch the video on the resources page, make sure you do, as it talks about one of the first ways to validate your idea using Amazon.

What the video shows you is how you can quickly validate your topic by visiting the Amazon Kindle store, checking out the Best Sellers and navigating to where your book idea would sit in the categories shown.

If you see similar books (in the categories shown) to your topic idea, then this is the first green light.

Look for at least 3 similar books in the top 20-40 best sellers.

Grab a pen and take note of the following:
1. Number of reviews the book has
2. What categories the book is ranked in
3. The rank of the book in the paid Kindle store
4. What type of cover they have (photo or illustrated?)
5. How much the book costs

What this tells you is that if there are 3 similar books in your niche, then you know that people are buying, particularly if they are in the top 20 (first page of best sellers in your category).

From there, using the paid Kindle rank, go to www.kdpcalculator.com and enter that number into the blank box shown - the result will tell you how many books the author is selling on average, per day.

A good book will average between 5-10 sales per day, once it's settled down following its publish date and first 30 days on Kindle.

Step 2 - Validate your topic on Amazon WITH KindleSpy

The next phase in this step is to use another tool called Kindle Spy – I find this tool helpful to quickly see what the top 20 Best Sellers are making from a money viewpoint, and it also provides you with a quick word cloud of the what the top 20 Best Sellers are using in their titles and subtitles.

This makes it a great option to delve in a bit further to see what the actual figures are. Kindle Spy is not free, but for the price of $37, I feel it's money well spent.

Step 3 - Validate your topic WITH KindleTrend

But you don't want to stop there, you need to validate your idea even further. To do this, you can use another great tool called KindleTrend (https://www.kindletrend.com/app/) - you can get memberships starting at $97 per month.

Watch the video (on the Resources page) on how I used KindleTrend to figure out why one of my current book's wasn't a good fit for Kindle and how I validated a book idea.

You don't NEED KindleTrend or Kindle Spy, but if you want to triple check your book ideas and make sure that you're going to be putting your best foot forward, then I highly recommend them.

What to do if you're bootstrapping:
If you don't want to spend any money at this stage, that's totally fine. Here's what you need to do to get the same validation as above using the paid tools.

1. Follow step 1 above and use the Amazon Best Sellers to determine if your idea is worth investigating further
2. Instead of just checking out 3 books though, you want to record information for all 20 in the Best Sellers list for your category
3. Use www.kdpcalculator.com to determine if any of these authors are making money (looking for 5-10 sales per day)
4. If you see more than 10 books in a category (in the best sellers) that fall higher than 20,000 in the paid Kindle store, then this is not a good niche to get into, i.e. your idea has not been validated.
5. If you see more than 10 books in a category (in the best sellers) that fall lower than 5,000 in the paid

Kindle store, then this niche is very competitive and will take a bit of work to rank in. If the top 3 books fall lower than 5,000 I'd personally walk away, unless you're an authority on the subject.

6. You are looking for 10 or so books (in the best sellers) that are between 5,000 - 20,000 in the paid Kindle store - this validates your niche and ensures that there is room to move in terms of competition.

Before you take any further steps, let's do a gut check—how are you feeling right now? Overwhelmed? Confused? I understand. It's a lot of information to take in.

Don't get too hung up on the details - validating your ideas shouldn't take you more than a couple of hours, even less if you go with the tools I recommend you use.

The Exception to the Rule: if you 'FEEL' that your idea is worth it, despite the validation process saying that it isn't, and you're prepared to put in some work to get the book noticed, then by all means, go ahead!

What I recommend you do right now is put down your Kindle or Kindle app (or paperback if you've got the paperback version) and take five.

Let things sink in a little, and then return with a fresh mind...

Welcome back! Are you all set to continue? Rested, relaxed

and ready to take in what you need to learn to make some extra income writing ebooks? Good, let's move on and start writing that book. Turn the page to make sure you've got all the steps sorted and check things off as you go.

Step 1 - Action List

AT THE end of each step, you're going to find a quick check list of things to do. Ideally, you should aim to to complete these steps BEFORE you move onto the next step, however, you know you best, so do what works best for you.

:: Checklist

- Review your idea in Amazon reviewing the Best Seller's in the category your idea would fit in
- 3 or more books in your category —> ok to move forward (less than this, back to the drawing board)
- Use KindleSpy to further validate your idea by seeing what the best sellers in that category are averaging money wise and where they rank in the paid Kindle store
- Take it a step further and use KindleTrend to confirm keyword ideas and run some more numbers
- If you're bootstrapping, do all of this manually as per the outlined instructions

You want to ensure that your book has the best chance to make you money. Validate your idea properly and I guarantee that your book will make at least $300 in its first month (at a minimum!).

Make sure you've ticked all of this off before moving to Step 2.

Ready to move on? Congratulations! You've come far and achieved some great things. The next few steps are going to blow your mind, so grab a cup of coffee and some pen and paper, and let's get cracking! Turn the page to learn how to write an ebook in just 4 short weeks!

4. Step 2 - Write a book in 4 weeks

Mind Mapping

BEFORE YOU start writing, you need to figure out what you're going to write! It's not enough to have just picked a book topic and then start writing, you need to solidify what you're going to write about too. You need a plan.

Before we delve in too much further, I'd like to point out that the majority of information I'm providing throughout this book is generally applicable to non-fiction writers.

If you're a fiction writer, writing a novel in 4 weeks might be a stretch if this is your side hustle! However, if you can write short novella's instead (think 20,000 - 60,000 words) then what I'm about to share with you will also apply to you too.

Here's the steps to take BEFORE you start to write.

Step 1 – Mind map your book idea

Rather than just jump straight into writing your book, it pays to provide yourself with a bit of a plan of how you're going to attack this process. I don't know about you, but I find it pretty difficult to just sit down and start writing without some sort of guide - if I want the writing to be good that is.

This is why, before you even start the writing process, you need to mind map your book idea. You should do this whether your book is fiction or non-fiction.

I know there are plenty of mind mapping tools available, but to be honest, I find that putting pen to paper 'releases' the flow of ideas more so than using an online tool or app. So I would highly recommend that you go this route too.

I like to use a large piece of poster sized paper and go nuts about my topic. I call it my 'brain fart'. No self editing is allowed during this step.

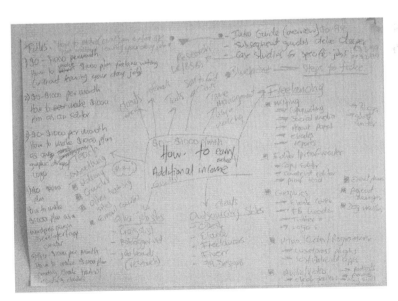

I put my book topic in the middle of the page, use a couple of different colored markers and go crazy with my writing.

I create ideas all over the place. The bigger the piece of paper, the more space I have and the bigger my writing gets.

I recommend you take a couple of hours to do this, as well as doing it over a couple of days, preferably the weekend. This allows your mind to think of more ideas and if you're writing fiction, it allows you to develop characters and worlds a bit more.

Step 2 – Organise similar ideas

Once you've got your initial mind map completed, you want to organize your ideas a bit more. To do this, I normally take another poster sized piece of paper and group similar ideas together and start to form chapter (or scenes for fiction) ideas.

These are not set in stone, so don't worry too much about how you label them. The whole point of this exercise is to make sure you're not doubling up or repeating yourself BEFORE you start writing.

I find it quite easy to go from my initial mind map to organizing similar ideas because I can 'see' the similar ideas laid out in front of me. I'm a visual person so this process really unlocks creativity. If this is something that doesn't work for you, go with your gut and organize your ideas how you see fit.

Step 3 – Outline your book

Once you've been through the mind mapping phase, you're now ready to outline your book, organize your chapters and start writing!

I like to us Evernote (www.evernote.com) to outline my books and I also use it to capture research and further ideas about each book I write.

If you're not familiar with Evernote, it's free, easy to install and you can get up and running quickly. Make sure you create a new notebook for each book you write, this will help keep things organized.

I normally scan my mind maps and add them to Evernote as well, so I can use my iPad as my second screen while I write. If you're used to working with two screens, I highly recommend doing this. It helps to be able to view your ideas during the writing phase in this way.

Now, you want to take your second mind map and start organizing the ideas into chapters within Evernote. Create a new note for each chapter heading and enter in all the ideas from your mind map here.

You can also add information, like what further research you need to do, what images you need, and what links you want to include. From there, you can create a high-level outline (all your chapters).

Step 4 – Choose your writing tool

You're nearly ready to start writing. It's important to note that the whole process outlined above should only take you 4 days max, dedicating 1-2 hours each session. If you want to fast-track these steps, doing so over a weekend is ideal.

Before you start writing, you need to choose your tool. If you prefer to write using pen and paper first, then jump to the next section "Writing the Write Way" now. If you prefer to type, read on.

I'm going to be blunt here - if you want to make a serious go at being an ebook writer, you need to learn how to use Scrivener (https://www.literatureandlatte.com/trial.php). Scrivener is the ONLY tool you should ever use to write any book with. Yes, you can use MS Word or Google Docs, but both of these will cause you major headaches when you get further down the track and ready to publish your book.

Take my word on this - Scrivener is your best option. The

price for this tool is $40, but you can trial it for 30 actual days of use. What this means is that if you OPEN it every day for 30 days, that's your trial period completed. But if you only open it 2 days per week, your trial period will last for 15 weeks. So you can see how you can use this without having to pay for it initially.

If you want a quick crash course on how to use Scrivener, watch the videos on the Resources Page. Scrivener has a bit of a learning curve, but if you can dedicate the time (2-3 hours) to learn what you need to know, it will be your hero further down the track.

You'll find a quick-start guide on how to get writing (quickly) with Scrivener also on the Resources Page.

If you don't want to learn something new, I get it and I understand - go ahead and use MS Word or Google Docs - but you've been warned...

In the next section, I'm going to provide you with advice on where you should start your actual writing process and we'll talk about your writing schedule and dealing with your little inner demon; your inner writing critic. Turn the page to get started.

Writing the Write Way

NOW THAT you've got your book outlined and have an idea of what your chapters are going to look like, you need to do one more thing before you start writing - research.

You might have already started grabbing things you need, but if you haven't, you need to do this now.

And the best way to do this is to grab the research you need at the beginning of the writing of each chapter. What do I mean by this?

It's simple. As you start your writing process, look at the chapter notebook in Evernote that you're writing about. What research items do you need? Go and grab the links to them and add into your chapter notebook just before you start writing that chapter. This ensures that everything you've seen is fresh in your mind.

So to reiterate and make myself clear, you want to research each chapter as you go.

A Word of Warning: Whatever you do, DO NOT plagiarize the information you read. Provide the appropriate credit where it's due and where possible, rewrite in your own words.

Ok, now you're ready to start writing!

Write what you know first

If you have personal experience with your non-fiction topic, then it makes sense to write the chapters you know the most about first.

If you're writing fiction, you can do the same here. If you've already got a few characters sussed out and some scene ideas in place, run with those first.

These are your quick wins. You want to start your book off with a few quick wins so that your brain can see something happening and so you feel rewarded and confident that things are coming together.

Writing can provide a bit of a mental block at times, so I find that if I start with the easy wins, it sets me up to write better. I know it will do the same for you too.

Set your deadline

We're sticking to a 4-week deadline here, and this starts the minute you start outlining your book. At the end of this chapter you'll find my 'Write a book in 4-weeks' calendar so that you can track your own progress against it.

So, set your deadline. You need to write to a deadline,

otherwise this will go on forever. You'll need to be writing for at least 1 hour per day, or writing at least 1,500 words per day - so work out which one is your measurement and go from there.

If you followed the KindleTrend video, you should have a rough idea of how long your book should be. For most non-fiction books, you want to be aiming for around 70-100 Kindle pages which is about 15,000 - 25,000 words.

If you're writing a novella, make sure you've checked out your genre and determine how many pages is optimal in that genre. Then work backwards and figure out how many hours you need to be writing to hit your deadline.

I know fiction writing is a little different, so if you find it works better to write in larger chunks of time, i.e., on the weekends, then do that.

The same applies to anyone that's writing non-fiction - if you'd rather sit down and write for 4-5 hours straight, then by all means do that. Do what works for you, but know what your schedule will be and what your target word count is so you know how you will hit your deadline.

Now I know you've probably got a million thoughts going around in your head and one of those is likely to be your inner critic. Turn the page to find out how to deal with any negativity you might feel towards your writing.

The Writing Mindset

"DONE IS better than perfect." This phrase is something I remind myself of every time I start to write a new book.

Side Note: I know that most of us like to edit as we go, but if you can resist doing that, you'll get your book completed within the 4-week period without too many headaches.

Now, how do you deal with your inner critic, that inner voice that won't shut up? There are many strategies that I use, and depending on how you like to work, some of these may or may not work for you. Try them all then decide which you like best.

Strategy 1 - Find an accountability partner

If you need to be held accountable, then find someone that WILL hold you accountable. Share with them your writing schedule and get them to check-in with you daily to see if you've meet your goals for that day. They can also be a buffer for your 'inner critic' negative talk and reassure you that you're doing great.

I find this worked extremely well for my first few books, but now that I've got the writing habit well and truly ingrained, I no longer need this.

This works well if you are both holding each other accountable. The other person doesn't need to be writing a book, but they do need to have some goals with deadlines in place so that you can hold them accountable too.

If you can't find an accountability partner, send me an email (lise@outsourcedfreelancingsuccess.com) and I can help find one for you!

Strategy 2 - Set reminders

Part of dealing with your inner critic lies in making sure that you are always hitting your mark, particularly if you plan to write for at least an hour each day. Starve your inner critic by setting reminders at certain times of the day when you plan to write.

This way you can ensure that you not only meet your goals, but you squash your inner critic from berating you for not writing or meeting your goals for that day.

Strategy 3 - Write like it's your job

This is something I learned early on, particularly if you're looking to do this on a more full-time basis further down the track. Pretend, when you sit down to write, that this is part of your 'normal' job and you'll find it far easier to get into the mindset of writing.

I'm not saying it's easy, but if you can tell yourself that and set yourself up in a space that feels like 'work' then you'll achieve this much faster.

Strategy 4 - Meditate for 5 minutes

This is something I've recently started implementing myself and works perfectly if you prefer to write first thing in the morning. Here's what you need to do:

1. Find a quiet space by yourself
2. Sit on the floor, with your legs crossed - sit on a pillow if the floor is uncomfortable
3. Close your eyes and start counting to 10 slowly, clearing your mind and just focusing on the counting
4. If you think about anything else other than the counting, you need to restart your counting from the beginning
5. Repeat until you can count continuously without thinking of anything else

Simple, but effective. Set your timer for 5 minutes and see how long it takes for you to clear your mind. This is probably the most effective way to get into the writing mindset. This is also an effective way to shut up the inner critic voice you'll start to hear the minute you start to write.

Strategy 5 - Tell your inner critic to take a

hike

This might seem simple, but it is VERY effective. The minute that you hear your inner critic giving you negative feedback or telling you that you can't write etc, acknowledge the voice and then politely (or not!) tell it to take a hike. You don't need to listen to this voice, so tell it to bugger off!

Between these five strategies, you'll squash any issues you have with your inner voice, and if you struggle with any of them, just keep at them for 30 days until it becomes second nature.

On the next page, you'll be able to see the calendar I use to write a book in 4 weeks. You can also access a printable version on the Resources page (link located in Chapter 12 - What's Next). Turn the page now to see the calendar!

Write a Book in 4-Weeks

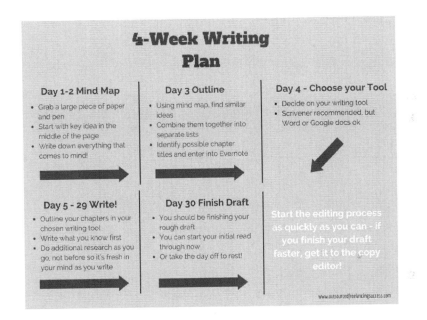

YOU'LL find a downloadable copy of the Writing Plan on the Resources Page as well. This is so you can print it off and stick it on your wall and refer back to it as you write.

Step 2 - Action List

REMEMBER, THIS checklist is here to ensure that you don't forget anything and that you follow the process. If you get stuck, circle back to the previous step.

:: Checklist

- Mind map your idea - do not skip this step - you'll regret it!
- Organize your ideas into similar ideas (forming chapter beginnings)
- Outline your book - this is your chapters
- Decide on your writing tool (learn Scrivener if you need to)
- Set your writing schedule (will you write in the morning, afternoon, evenings? For how long?)
- Set a deadline to have your first draft completed
- Deal with any mindset issues you have by implementing one of the strategies
- Review the calendar and print it off to make sure you're on track

In the next chapter, I'm going to share with you how to edit the book yourself and then at what point you need to hand it off to an editor. I'll also walk you through how to find a good editor and why you cannot edit your book alone, even if you're an editor in your day job! Turn the page to get started.

5. Step 3 - Editing

Self Editing

CONGRATULATIONS! YOU'VE written your first draft and you're now ready to kick things into gear.

The editing phase is done in three parts: self-editing, content editing and copy editing. All three phases are different and the following information should be followed to ensure that you have a book that you're proud of and, most importantly, that is easy to read and will make you some money!

Phase 1 – Self Editing

Allow yourself a few days to complete this. If you're using Scrivener, as I did, then turn on 'Revision Mode' choosing the 'first revision' option, which is a nice red for easy identification. In MS Word, turn on 'Track Changes' and if you're using Google Docs, turn on your 'Editing' mode.

You will find Revision Mode located under 'Format' in the top menu drop down box. Once turned on, it's applied to your entire document. You can tell that it's on in two ways:

1. When you type, the words are in red, and

2. The text color option displays as red

During the self-editing phase, I find that I tend to get rid of quite a bit of fluff – sentences and paragraphs that don't add to the book in any way. You should aim to do the same. One of the easiest ways to identify 'fluff' is to read through your book from cover to cover, but read it out loud. If you stumble over any words or phrases, then these are the ones you'll want to remove or reword.

I also look for filler words, words that don't add to the meaning of a sentence or phrase. For example, when you're writing a first draft, you'll probably find that you overuse the words "very" and "the" a lot. By removing them, you instantly improve the quality of your writing and your book by a good 30-40 percent.

Follow these quick tips when self-editing:

1. Remove fluff content – anything that isn't important or required to get the point across
2. Remove filler words – words like "very" and "the" are good examples
3. Add stories to help illustrate your points where needed

This last point is important. If you're writing non-fiction, you need to be able to connect with your audience. Telling stories helps to do this and also illustrates your points further. Of course, if you're writing a fiction book, this goes without saying, you're telling stories left, right and center!

When I wrote my books, "No Gym Needed," I had plenty of stories to add to the books because I was writing from personal experience – everything that I wrote in the books really did happen! Oh the shame... 😀 If you haven't read them yet, make sure you check them out here - lisecartwright.com/books-by-lise/!

Once you've done this first phase in self-editing, you need to run it through an app that I love, particularly from a non-fiction writing point of view.

The Hemingway App

This app (www.hemingwayapp.com/) will tell you if your grammar is crap, identify spelling mistakes, highlight sentence difficulty from a reading point of view plus so much more. It will force you to simplify your sentences, depending on who your target audience is.

It works for both fiction and non-fiction books. You can use it for free on the web, or your can get the pro version for $6.99 which allows you to download the desktop app. Choose what works best for you.

A word of caution: as you go through the app, if something doesn't feel right to you, don't change it. Your editor will let you know if it works or not. The Hemingway

App is just a great way to tidy up your work before you hand it over to an editor.

Once you've completed the self-editing phase, you're ready to unleash the book out into the world and get some much needed feedback...

On the next page, you'll learn how you can get access to some content editors for free or how you can hire someone to do the whole editing process for you from 'woh to go.' Turn the page to find out more.

Content Editing

BEFORE WE jump into the rest of the editing phases, let's look at the two different types of editors that you could potentially end up hiring, depending on your book genre.

1. Content Editor:
What is a content editor? It's having someone read through your book and make sure that the content you've written makes sense, flows well and is factual (important for non-fiction books, not so much for fiction). It helps to have someone who also knows your topic well to do a content edit for you.

2. Copy Editor:
A copy editor is someone who will edit your book from a grammar and sentence structure perspective. They'll also make sure that the formatting is the same across the book and make sure that your book makes sense. In most instances, they won't know much about your content, so they can't provide advice from that perspective, unless you hire a content AND copy editor that is. Think of them as a proof reader with superhero qualities!

Right, now that you understand the difference between the two, let's start with next phase of the editing process.

Phase 2 – Content Editing

There are two ways you can go about getting content editing done:

1.   Pay for a content and copy edit at the same time, or
2.   Ask friends or people you know well to read it for you. You can also find someone that knows your subject well, like someone in your network.

Avoid asking any of your colleagues to help with this, particularly if you don't want them to know what you're up to with your side hustle.

If you don't want to spend too much time on this part of the editing phase, ask some good friends to do the content edit for you. If you have an accountability partner, this person is definitely a good option for your content editor. Keep in mind that if your book is long (i.e. Is fiction and over 30, 000 words) a friend is going to take a good week to provide this edit for you.

Ideally, you want your content edit to be done within 2-3 days.

Get these people to provide you with some very specific feedback:

1.   Ask them whether the content makes sense and flows well from a readability point of view

2. Ask them if what you've written is factual (mainly non-fiction writers)
3. Ask them if I you've missed anything out/or need to add more information (get them to be specific)
4. Ask them what their thoughts are around the way the book is currently structured, and should you move chapters around?

It's important that if you are getting the content and copy edit done separately that you remind your content editor(s) not to focus on grammar and spelling, as the copy editor will do that.

When I wrote my first few books, I gave my content editors a MS word document, with 'track changes' turned on in so that I could see where they made changes and so they could also provide comments directly within the document.

I exported the file out of Scrivener into Word for this process. You will want to do the same.

To learn how to do this, watch the video on the Resources Page - "How to Compile into Word from Scrivener."

This part of the editing process is important - failure to do this could lead to your book bombing big time. You can make major changes at this stage of your editing process - you can't once it's been professionally edited, without it costing you MUCH MORE money. We want to avoid this at all costs.

On the next page we are going to move into the final phase of the editing process - handing your prized document over to a copy editor. This part is scary - I'm not gonna lie. But it is necessary. If you've run your book through the Hemingway App and through the content edit process, it should be at a pretty good stage. If you don't do either of these and hand it to a copy editor straight from the get go - you may face some issues. So don't skip these phases!

Turn the page to get started on the final editing phase.

Copy Editing

RIGHT, LET'S get straight into it!

Phase 3 - Copy Editing

The copy editing phase is one of THE most important aspects of producing a quality ebook. If your copy is riddled with spelling and grammar mistakes, even if your content is good, it will turn readers off.

It makes it difficult to read a book if you're having to stop and rewrite a word or sentence in your head as you're reading!

Unfortunately, this part of the phase requires you to spend some money. You can't get around not having an editor do this for you. If you have a friend that is great with grammar and you trust them, then they offer a good solution for anyone that is bootstrapping.

Everyone else, follow my guidelines on how to hire an editor without it costing you loads of money.

There are some specific questions to ask when looking to hire someone to do this, particularly around getting a good price and stipulating deadlines.

The best place to look to hire someone is checking out sites like oDesk or Elance, with my preference being Elance.

I'm not going to go into detail about how you post a job on Elance or oDesk, once you sign up to either of those sites, it's pretty self explanatory about what you need to do.

What I am going to provide you with is a template you can use to post your job.

Side note: If you want to hire both a content and copy editor at the same time, make sure you include a bit more information about the topic of your book, and that you'd like someone with prior knowledge in that topic to do the edit for you.

Sample Job Description Template:
"I need a copy editor (read - someone to proofread for spelling and grammar errors) to edit my [xxx word] MS word document, utilising track changes.

Include this sentence if no formatting required: No formatting required, just a straight proofread for spelling and grammar errors - spelling should be [US based.]

Include this sentence if formatting is required: Please ensure that the formatting of the document is consistent throughout, proofread for spelling and grammar errors as well as sentence structure. Spelling should be [US based.]

I need this completed by [Sunday, 19th October.]"

————

Anything that's in square brackets needs to be changed to suit your requirements.

As an example on pricing, my No Gym Needed books sat around the 25,000 word mark when it was sent to the copy editor. The quotes I received for that word count were between $300-$400.

This might seem like a lot of money, but consider that you could lose even more than that if your book is hard to read, and you can see the value in paying someone to do the job properly.

You can find cheaper editors, just make sure that they have some previous work to show you before you hire them. Always trust your instinct and if you're not sure, ask them to do a sample edit for you.

DO NOT think you can edit the book yourself – you will miss spelling mistakes and grammar issues easily, particularly if you've read through the document a few times.

Our brains are clever – they will turn misspelled words into what they should be when we're reading, particularly if it's our own work.

Don't make this mistake – you won't make any money on Kindle or any other platform with poorly written ebooks.

If you're bootstrapping, plead with a friend to do the editing for you, utilizing the help of the Hemingway App - just be warned that this is not the ideal scenario for a professionally written ebook.

This whole process (self-editing, content and copy editing) should take no more than 2 weeks (maximum), depending on the length of your book.

Once your editor has the book, if you haven't determined your book title, now is the time to get that sorted.

Developing a book title

I won't go into this part in too much detail, because it could be a whole book on its own! What I will say is that you need to think about a few different aspects when choosing a book title and subtitle, regardless of whether you're writing fiction or non-fiction:

- What keywords (from your niche/category) are most used by best sellers inside the Kindle/Kobo/Nook store?
- Who is your target audience? Can you include them in your title or subtitle?
- Try and use present tense and active voice –

negative words and passive voice don't sell books

I struggled with my No Gym Needed book title and subtitle initially. I got hung up on the working title I'd been using up until that point, which was "No-Gym Workouts". I liked the way it sounded and it explained the book to a "T", or so I thought!

At this stage of the writing process, I hadn't planned on doing two books. The original idea for the NGN book was to aim it at both men and women and it wasn't until I got to the title stage that I realized that I would be better targeting the book to women first and then following up with a male version soon after, which is what I did.

This one decision greatly affected this book's direction, which helped me develop a title and subtitle that made sense. It also caused a few issues for my editor, as I had to stop her mid-way through the editing process, because I needed to rework the book to be focused on women.

Lesson learned – make sure you're clear on your target audience BEFORE you hand it to the editor!

From there, I went to Facebook and asked for feedback on three different title and subtitle options. Doing this helped me further develop the title and led me to what I now have for the women's version – "No Gym Needed: Quick and Simple Workouts for Gals on the Go. Get a Toned Body in 30 Minutes or Less!"

This is also a 'sneaky' marketing tactic - make note of it and we'll come back to it later in Step 5 - Book Launch.

Once you've got the title and subtitle nailed down, it's time to look at your cover and book design options. This part of the process can start while your book is with the editor, so don't think you can take a break, particularly if you want to make $1000 per month out of this side hustle!

On the next page, you'll find a checklist to ensure that you don't miss any of the important aspects of the editing phase. Turn the page to learn more.

Step 3 - Action List

REMEMBER, THIS checklist is here to ensure that you don't forget anything and that you follow the process. If you get stuck, circle back to the previous step.

:: Checklist

- Read your book through from cover to cover, making sure that you read it out loud so you can catch any fluff or filler words
- Remove fluff and filler words discovered
- Run your book through the Hemingway App and make any necessary changes
- Have your book run through a content edit - utilize your network first, then look to hire someone (as a last resort)
- Make any changes to your book based on the comments from your content editor feedback
- Hire a copy editor using the template provided - make sure you confirm pricing and deadlines
- Hand your book over to the copy editor
- Finalise your title and subtitle

In the next section, we're going to focus on the design of your book - I highly recommend not getting your editor to format your book for you, particularly if you're going to use Scrivener. If you're not using Scrivener, then formatting by your editor is ok, but I'd still advise against it. Turn the page to find out why!

6. Step 4 - Design

Book Design

WHEN IT comes to formatting the interior of your book, personally, I feel that Scrivener is by far the best way to go. Your editor should NOT be doing this for you - their focus should be on making sure your book reads properly, not how pretty it looks.

The bottom line on book formatting, particularly if you have a fiction book, is that you want to keep it as simple as possible. Think about where the end product finishes up - on an e-reader, like a Kindle, iPad etc. And in most cases, people prefer to read their books in black and white.

When I write a book, here's the formatting 'standards' I use throughout:

1. Font size = 14
2. Spacing = 1.2
3. Font = basic like Times New Roman, Calibri, Arial etc (only basic fonts are supported on e-reader apps)
4. Main headings = Font + 18 point size + bold
5. Sub Headings = Slightly different font + 16 point + bold
6. Bullet or numbered lists

I don't worry about highlighting text, coloring text or anything else. Simplicity is key to making your words stand out.

The best way to emphasize word's or phrases throughout your text is to put them in italics or indent them. Just keep it simple so that whatever device your end reader views it on, it translates well enough.

If you've followed my advice and have been using Scrivener, there are loads of different things you can do to format your book once you're at the 'compile' stage. I won't go into too much detail about that, but if you want a comprehensive tutorial on how to format your book using Scrivener, you'll find one on the Resources Page.

The best part about using Scrivener is that it converts straight to a .mobi or .epub file. This means that you can miss out the middle man and create the publish-ready file yourself.

It will create a clickable table of contents for you as well AND it can even create the NCX table of contents for the Kindle app. This is what you can see when you view your book in the Kindle app and click on the three lines at the top that pops out options, one of which is your table of contents.

If you're using anything other than Scrivener, then your

best bet is to apply no formatting at all and pay for someone to do this for you.

While it's true that Kindle will accept a MS Word document to upload, if you do this without first having it converted to a .mobi file, you'll encounter a whole host of formatting issues.

Fiverr (www.fiverr.com) is your best place to go to have someone format your Word document for .mobi conversion. Just make sure that you provide them with specific details about what you want, or you could see yourself end up in a back and forth email exchange... Again, use the KISS principle above and keep it simple.

When working with an outsourcer, whether on Fiverr or Elance, make sure that you check to ensure that you get at least 1-2 revisions included in the price. There are bound to be a few errors and you don't want to have to pay for a tweak every time you spot one. You'll find a sample outline of what you can provide to an outsourcer on the Resources Page, should you need one.

While you're busy formatting your book, you should have someone else working on the cover design for you so that this process is done in tandem. You don't want to be waiting around for your cover.

In the next section, we're going to look at how you can get your cover done cheaply or if you want to ensure your books success, how to properly brief a more expensive designer. Turn the page to learn more!

Cover Design

WHILE YOU'RE figuring our your book formatting and structure, you should be outsourcing your cover design. Now, unless you're a graphic artist yourself, DO NOT try and do your book cover yourself. If you are bootstrapping, I get it, but this part of the process is one where you do not want to cut corners on.

Below are some options to consider when it comes to getting your book cover designed properly. I'll start with the least expensive and end on the most expensive. The choice is yours.

Fiverr

Fiver is by far the least expensive way to go. For $5 you can have someone design your book cover, in fact, I'd recommend getting at least 4 different covers designed so that you've got a few options to choose from and compare across the different designers.

If you're going the Fiverr route, consider these points first:

- Have a few ebook covers that you already like handy
- Know what you don't want
- Decide on your colors before hiring someone, or at

least have a color palette/range in mind
- Decide whether you want photos or graphics (you may need to purchase these)

The more information you can provide to the designer, the closer they'll get to what you want. Fiver is NOT a good option if you have no idea what you're looking for.

Choose one of the other options if this is you, or you could find yourself spending money trying to find the right book designer.

Etsy

I stumbled across a few designers on Etsy when I was looking for a gift for my best friend's baby shower. Etsy is definitely not the first place I would have looked, but you'd be surprised at what you can find on Etsy.

Typically, a book cover designed on Etsy can range anywhere from $25-$125, so it does pay to shop around. I found a great designer on here, but unfortunately, she is no longer taking on any work.

Here are a couple of designers to check out instead:

- Custom eBook Cover Designs
- eBook Covers

What I like about Etsy is that this is a good option if you want to spend more than $5 and ensure you get something that looks professional. In most cases, they'll allow a few revisions for the price quoted and you get high-resolution images and PDF's with some even offering the PSD file.

I'd recommend that you ask for the PSD file (you'll have to pay extra) if you're planning to do a series of books. This is just in case the designer is not available the next time you're ready for a book cover in that series. It pays to plan ahead...

Elance/oDesk

You can find a huge range of graphic designers on both these sites. It will take some time to wade through the people that submit their proposal, unless you specifically pick 10 candidates and invite them to apply and make your ad visible only to them. This is how I would recommend you approach either of these sites, otherwise you will be completely overwhelmed with applications.

Ideally, you'd want to find someone who is in a similar or comparable timezone so that if you need quick revisions, they can be done in real-time.

On my last book, the Side Hustle Blueprint - Book 1, my book publish date was held up because of my cover designer and that was largely due to timezone differences. While he is great, being in a timezone that doesn't quite gel with mine lead to unnecessary delays that could have been avoided had I been working with someone locally or someone that was a bit closer.

99Designs

This is the biggie. 99Designs is for designers to showcase their work to potential buyers with one key difference - you place a job and freelancers bid on your job, providing their ideas upfront. This could mean that you have 30 book cover options to choose from!

Personally, I find that quite overwhelming and this goes into the 'too hard' basket as far as I'm concerned. I like to keep things simple and generally, I need to move quickly with designs.

99Designs is ideal if you have a bit more time, a bit more moola and are looking to create a real brand for yourself. Packages start at $299 so this is definitely not for anyone looking to bootstrap their Kindle empire!

Other Options

If you're really struggling financially and just find Fiverr confusing, there is another option for you, but this is a last resort option, ok?

Visit www.canva.com and use the Kindle ebook cover template they have. Choose one of the predesigned ones and then make it work for your book.

You might be able to get away with this if you have a few covers you like open on Kindle - why reinvent the wheel when there are so many covers that already do so well?

On the next page, you'll find a checklist to ensure that you don't miss any of the important aspects of the design phase. Turn the page to learn more.

Step 4 - Action List

REMEMBER, THESE checklists are here to ensure that you don't forget anything and that you follow the process. If you get stuck, circle back to the last step or back to the beginning and just start again.

:: Checklist

- Format your book, ensuring to keep it simple
- Source some covers you like
- Decide on what outsourcing option your going to go with for your book cover design
- Place an ad and wait for responses or purchase the gig on Fiverr or Etsy
- Ensure you read the fine print in any proposals before hiring someone

In the next chapter, we're going to look at how you should best launch and market your book. Without proper pre-thought at this point, your book could completely fail. Turn the page to learn how to avoid having this happen to you.

7. Step 5 - Book Launch

Pre-Launch Phase

ONCE YOU'VE got your final copy finished and your cover design all done, you're ready to enter the book launch phase. There are three main parts to the book launch phase:

1.   Pre-Launch Phase
2.   Launch Phase
3.   Post-Launch Phase

In this section, we're going to cover the pre-launch phase. You want to set yourself up for success, so it's important that you follow through on what's outlined here.

Prior to the pre-launch phase you need to upload your finished book to KDP (Kindle Direct Publishing). And while this process is fairly straight-forward, there are a few parts of the process that can trip you up.

Let's get straight into it!

KDP Upload

5 days prior to your launch date, you'll want to upload your book to KDP. Don't do this any earlier, as it will lesson the amount of time your book can appear in the "Hot New Releases" list. You only get 30 days in this list, so you want to maximize it as much as possible.

First things first. Do you have a KDP account? If you've never self-published a book before (and I'm guessing you haven't if you're reading this book) then you need to do this first. If you already have an Amazon account, you can log in with those details.

Navigate your way to the following URL: https:// kdp.amazon.com/. Either sign up or log in with your Amazon account details. You'll be presented with the following screen (without any books of course!):

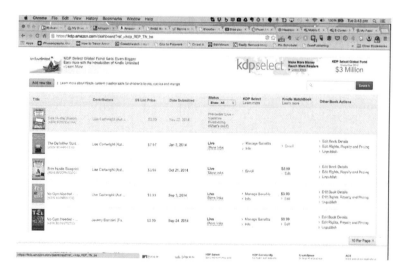

This is your KDP dashboard. You'll get pretty familiar with it the more books you write, but for now, just make sure that you're on this screen.

You'll see a button on the left hand side of the screen that says "Add a new title" - click this and follow the steps to upload your book. Make sure you tick "enrol book in KDP Select."

Below are the areas that you need to focus on to make sure you have a successful book launch:

Book Description
Unfortunately (fortunately?), this is where you need to write some compelling sales copy. I know it's not super comfy doing this for the first time, but it does get easier the more you do it. To nail your book description, look at some similar books on Amazon and see what they've got written for their book description.

I'm good at rewriting content and this is what I'd recommend you do with your first couple of book descriptions. Find one you like and then told it to fit your book.

If you're still stuck, here are a couple of my books for you to take a look at - feel free to use their descriptions as a base to start off from:

- No Gym Needed Book 1
- Side Hustle Blueprint Book 1

- <u>Guide to Freelance Writing Work on oDesk</u>

Once your book has been approved by KDP (typically takes 4-8 hours), you'll need to come back to this section and add some HTML tags to add in bold, italics and the 'Amazon Orange' heading. We want to make it look pretty.

You can find the list of HTML tags that will work in this area on the <u>KDP help centre</u>. If you're not sure how to do this at all, make sure you watch the video on the Resources Page.

Amazon Categories
Once you've finished with your book description, you need to choose two categories for your book. The aim here is to choose cross categories. This means that you should have your book showing up in two completely different main categories.

While this might not work for every book, it does work for most non-fiction books and even fiction books can capitalize on this by appearing in two different genre's.

A word of warning - the categories that you'll be presented with in the KDP back area don't necessarily match up with what you'll see when looking at books in the Kindle store on Amazon. I've no idea why Amazon have done this, and it definitely makes things confusing.

The best way to navigate your way through this is to have an idea of your categories BEFORE you start the KDP uploading process.

If you don't have any idea what categories your book would fit in, go back to Amazon and look at the Kindle store, focusing on the best sellers again. Find similar books to yours and see what categories they are in. Write these down and then come back to the KDP area and choose your two categories.

Keywords

Once you've chosen your categories, you have the ability to add 7 keywords into the KDP uploading area. For those of you familiar with basic search engine optimization principles, this is to help people find your book when they are searching on Amazon and Google to a lesser extent.

The best way to find your keywords is to go back to the research phase and look at what keywords you wrote down then. Use MerchantWords to help you further refine your keywords. You want to find keywords that are getting less than 5,000 searches per month.

Add these into the space provided by KDP, separating with a comma.

If you find this process overwhelming, make sure you watch the step-by-step video on how to upload to KDP on the Resources Page. The video walks you through this process, so you can follow along as you're doing it.

Cover Image and Book File

At this point you should still be on the first page of the KDP uploading process. Keep following along with the steps until you get to the point where you're ready to upload your cover image.

Upload the highest quality image of your cover that your designer provided to you. This is the cover that will be used in the Kindle store, so you want it to look good.

Once you've done this, you're ready to upload your actual book. Hopefully you've used Scrivener to convert your file to .mobi and you're ready to go.

Follow the steps to upload your file. Make sure you choose the right file and then upload it. It can take a good 5 minutes to upload. Amazon may prompt you to save your books progress at this point.

Once the books interior file has been uploaded, you'll get a message telling you that it was a success. It might also tell you that there are some spelling errors - check those and make sure they aren't actual spelling errors. If all is ok, proceed to the next page by clicking "Save and Proceed."

Book Pricing

The last part of the KDP process is to choose your pricing. As part of the pre-launch strategy that we're focusing on, you'll want to set your books initial price at around the $9.99 price point. This means that you'll be choosing the

70% commission payout. While you probably won't be selling your book at this price following your free promotion period, this is part of our pre-launch strategy.

If you have a fiction book, set your initial price point at around the $6.99 price point. This still falls within the 70% commission payout.

Allow Amazon to set the price for all countries. Scroll to the bottom and make sure you tick to include the book in Amazon's borrowing program. You still get paid if people borrow your book, so there's no harm in doing this.

You can also enrol the book in Amazon's match program - but only do this if you plan to publish your book on CreateSpace as a paperback. More on that later.

Right, that's KDP! Let's look at the rest of the pre-launch phase.

Where possible, you should be running parts of the pre-launch phase while you book cover design is being finalized, so they can be run congruently. You're about to see why!

The aim is to have your pre-launch phase run for two weeks prior to launch. It can be done in 5 days, but I'd recommend two weeks for your first book.

Pre-Launch Phase Steps

1. Book Cover Feedback

As you're deciding on your book cover, you want to start raising awareness of your impending book launch. The best way to do this is to get people to vote and provide feedback on your book cover via social media. Facebook and Pinterest work well for this. This is part of our 'sneaky' marketing tactics.

Aim to have 2-3 covers designed and then present these to your Facebook friends or on your Facebook page if appropriate.

Here's what you can say:

"I'm in the process of writing a new book which will be released on Amazon's Kindle store in the next few weeks and I could use your help! I've got 3 book covers and I'd love your help in choosing one. In the comments below, can you let me know which one you prefer? Thanks for your help!"

Make it more personal if you're posting on your personal Facebook page. Add the three images to the post and wait to see what happens.

If you don't want your friends and family to know what you're doing, Facebook groups are a great place to start. If you belong to a Facebook group that aligns with your book idea, then post something similar in there.

If you want feedback from other self-published author's, Pat Flynn of SmartPassiveIncome.com has a great community on Facebook (https://www.facebook.com/groups/357112331027292/#sthash.KtTel2yw.dpuf) that are active when it comes to providing feedback on book covers. Request to join and post in there as soon as you can. Make sure you also participate in a few posts first, this is good community karma.

2. Opt-in Page

This applies for both fiction and non-fiction books. You want to let as many people know about your upcoming book plus you want to start building an email list. The best way to do this is to set up a simple landing page to let people know how they can get on the 'early notification list' to get access to your book for FREE once it launches.

This is why you need to allow two weeks for your pre-launch. Below is a screenshot of the opt-in page I used for my first No Gym Needed book.

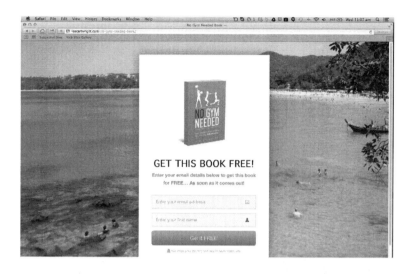

Side Note: yes, you are going to be launching your book for free for up to 5 days. I'll explain more about this below.

I use OptimizePress 2 on my websites because it provides these built in landing pages. OptimizePress is not cheap though. If you're bootstrapping, you can use a service like Instapage. You can access this for free or their paid service starts at $17.

You'll also need to connect this to a mail management service. I use MailChimp, but there are many different options. MailChimp provides a free service initially, and I highly recommend it. Watch their training video's if you've never set up an email management program before.

Once you're opt-in page is setup, share it like crazy. And not just once or twice, share it daily across all your social media networks. Ask others in your network to share it as well, after all, you're providing something for free so why wouldn't they want to share it.

3. Submit Your Book to Free Kindle Book Sites

This is a MUST if you want your book to be a success. If you don't have an email list at all, this is even more important. In most instances, these free sites work for both fiction and non-fiction books and *require at least 5-7 days notification* that you want to submit your book to them. This is why you need to have your book uploaded and 'live' on Amazon 5 days prior to your launch date.

You need your ASIN number and the direct link to your books page in order to submit to these sites. You can find your ASIN number directly under your title in your KDP Bookshelf (see below) and you'll find your direct link to your books page by hovering over the "store links" option (see below).

You'll find a list of all the free sites on the Resources Page. Give yourself a good 2 hours to do this, as it can take a bit of time!

4. Reviews

Part of a successful launch week is all in the reviews your

book has prior to the launch date. In fact, some of the submission sites above require you to have at least 5 positive reviews on your book!

There are a number of ways you can get reviews.

Here's what I recommend you do:

1. Ask your friends and family to leave an unverified review on your books page. This means that they haven't purchased the book. Amazon allows people to leave a review against a book or product without actually verifying you've purchased a book or product. This works well in your favor (for now - could change in the future).

2. Remember those Facebook Groups you belong to? Or Pat Flynn's Facebook Group? Offer to do a review exchange with other authors. This means that you'll give someone a copy of your book for free in exchange for a review and you'll also return the favor.

3. If you do have an email list and your book would be of interest to them, send them an email letting them know that you're looking for beta-readers. You'll give them a free copy of the book in exchange for a review on Amazon. If you're doing this, give them at least 7 days to read your book. Give them a deadline and if they can't meet that deadline, then don't give them the book.

The aim is to have 5-10 reviews on your book before your launch date.

And that concludes the pre-launch phase. There are a lot of moving parts, so I know it can be a lot to focus on. Which is why you'll find a launch plan at the end of this chapter (and for download from the Resources Page) - it tells you what to do when!

In the next section, we're going to look at the launch phase. It's make or break time. Let's launch that book - turn the page to get started.

Launch Phase

OK, IT'S crunch time. This is probably going to be the most nerve racking part of the process. Even more nerve racking than waiting to hear what your editor thought of your book.

It's launch week!

So, I'm not going to beat around the bush. Let's jump straight in and get this baby hitting the number 1 best seller list!

Setting Your Launch Day

There is a little bit of a debate around which days work best for launching a free book and so far, the best day appears to be a Sunday. Keep in mind that Amazon is based in Central Time (USA) so you need to base all your promotions around this timezone. Very tricky if you don't live in North America, but doable with a few tools. I personally use www.worldtimeclock.com and my iPhone's international clock options to figure this out.

2 days prior to your launch day, log into your KDP dashboard and look at your book title. You'll see a column titled "KDP Select" and in that column will be the option to "Manage Benefits" - click this and you'll be taken to the KDP select area, where you'll now choose your launch

dates.

The default option shown is a Countdown Deal - but you can't participate in this option until your book has been on the Kindle store for 30 days and remained the same price for 30 days. Click on the drop-down box and choose "Free Book Promotion" - then choose your dates. You can have up to 5 days in this promotion. This means that if you start your promotion on a Sunday, it will end on a Thursday.

Go ahead and choose your dates and then save those options. Remember, you need to do this at least 2 days before your actual launch date, otherwise it won't work.

Once you've got this sorted, the following process should be followed during your launch week:

Day 1: Your book is live and in it's first day on free promotion. Today you want to push for reviews. Send an email out to your early notification email list and let them know that the book is live and available for free download. Ask them to leave a review as well. This will get you your first verified reviews.

Day 2: Share your book on Facebook with your friends (if you want to) and any other groups you belong too. Share your book on the free Facebook Groups specifically for Kindle books. Create images to share on your other social media accounts as well. Make it fun. If you're launching a fiction book, take quotes from your book and match them with images. This is a great promotion strategy.

Day 3: Share your book on the free Facebook Groups specifically for Kindle books. You can find a list of these on the Resources Page. Continue to share your book, images and quotes across your social media networks.

Day 4: Continue promoting your book using suggestions from Day 2-3. However, if you're book has hit the Top 100 Free Kindle Store, then it's time to start monitoring it closely. If you start to see your book downloads start to slow or your book drops down a few spots in the Top 100 Free Kindle Store, it's time to end your promotion early. The key to a successful book launch is to manually end the book promotion between 12pm-3pm Central Time and switch your price to $0.99.

If your book is holding strong within the Top 100 Free Kindle Store, leave it in the promotion for another 12 hours.

Day 5: Promote your book in the morning and then end the book promotion early. Manually end the book promotion between 12pm-3pm Central Time and switch your price to $0.99. The reason for doing this is that it takes a while for Amazon to update it's records, so while that is happening, people can still be finding your book in the Free Kindle Store, but you're book is no longer free. At the price point of $0.99, people will still buy.

During your launch week, you can also run some paid advertising. This is completely optional. The service that I've found to be useful is a Tweeting service that promotes your book to fiction and non-fiction readers.

For one day, it will cost you $29 USD for 24 hours of tweets about your book. Tweet Your Books is a great service and I highly recommend using them.

The other thing you'll want to do during your books launch week is to take screenshots of your books stats.

These are the areas you want to focus on:

1. Downloads. You can see these in your KDP dashboard > Reports. Click the reports tab at the top and you'll be presented with a graph. This will tell you how many free downloads you've had each day (the green line).
2. Your Amazon Best Sellers Rank. You can see this on your books actual sales page on Amazon. You'll find this information under the "Product Details" area. It's about half way down your books sales page. I recommend taking a screenshot every few hours to track your progress each day!

Once your book switches to paid, you should still continue to track these two stats, except that instead of downloads, it will be sales and borrows that you're tracking (red and blue lines).

I also keep track of my books in a spreadsheet. Once you have more than once book published, it's important that you do this as each book you publish affects the other books you have published under that author name. You can find a copy of my spreadsheet on the Resources Page for your use.

Building Your Email List

Another way to build your email list is to offer a free incentive inside the first few pages of your book. For non-fiction books, I'd recommend some type of Action Guide that goes along with your book. This should also be a stand alone guide, as you'll also get sign ups from people that don't buy your book but access the first few pages of your book using the "Look Inside" feature that Amazon provides. So the action guide needs to be able to stand on it's own, without forcing people to buy your book (although most will).

I did this for both my No Gym Needed books and then for the first Side Hustle Blueprint book, I offered a *27 Tips & Hacks for Freelancers Guide*. This is a great way to build your email list without spending lots of dollars on advertising.

If you're book is a fiction book, have an audio version of your book as the freebie works well. You can also offer that as a giveaway in a non-fiction book as well. If an audio version isn't possible, fiction authors also have a lot of success giving away another fiction book, so if you have a short story or novella you could give away as your freebie, this would work well too.

And that's launch week done and dusted. Congratulations - you did it! You're now a self-published author.

Bask in your success for a few days then come back and find out how you can maintain your book sales and how you can turn this into an ongoing profitable business. Turn the page to learn more about the post-launch and monthly marketing phases.

Post-Launch Phase

CONGRATULATIONS ON launching your book! I bet you're feeling pretty great right now - you self-published your book and you hit #1 best seller status in your category. That's an amazing achievement.

Take some time to languish in that feeling and the knowledge that you actually did this!

Once you've done that, it's time to figure out how to maintain your sales. Where many self-published authors fail is in maintaining their book sales. They think that all they have to do is publish their book, share it a few times and hey presto, self-published millionaire... But, as I'm sure you're learning fast, this is NOT how it works.

You should be treating your ebook writing side hustle as a normal business. You have to continue to maintain and grow it, if you want to continue earning the moola!

With that said, let's look at our post-launch phase.

Post-Launch Phase Steps

You enter this phase as soon as you switch from free to paid. You want to continue to track your book, but instead of looking at downloads, you'll want to track sales and

Kindle Unlimited accesses (red and blue lines).

As I've mentioned already, the first 30 days of your book being published on Amazon will land it in the Hot New Releases list. So after your initial launch and marketing, you don't have to do anything else other than continue to share it on social media during this time.

Amazon will take care of the rest, highlighting your book in direct emails to interested buyers and showcasing your book in the categories it hit #1 in. It's after the first 30 days that you need to start looking at maintaining your book sales.

Here are some ideas around how you can do this:

1. Publish another book! This is by far the quickest way to increase sales on all your published books. It's also the best way to grow your self-publishing income. Aim to release a book a month for the next 12 months and you could be walking away from your full-time job, earning far more than you thought possible!

2. Write guest blog posts promoting your book. Find blogs that you can write for and provide a high-value blog post that has a call-to-action at the bottom promoting your book. Make sure the content of the blog post is relevant to the target audience. You can learn more about how to find and approach bloggers to guest post here (https://

blog.kissmetrics.com/guide-to-guest-blogging/).

3. Convert your Kindle book into a paperback using CreateSpace. It's free to do this and will increase your revenue. It will also increase Kindle sales as your paperback book will be higher priced and when you link your paperback book with your Kindle book (this is the Match program), it will show how much people save if they buy the Kindle book. It's a great tactic and who doesn't want to see their books in actual print?!

4. Convert your Kindle book into an audio book. If you haven't already done this as part of your free opt-in, you should definitely do this now. Audible is the audio book branch of Amazon and you can set this up without having to pay voice talent if you agree to share profits with them.

5. Jump on some podcasts and get yourself interviewed. This is surprisingly easier than it may sound. A lot of podcast hosts struggle to find people to interview. See if any of the blogs that you looked at for guest blogging also have a podcast. Send them an email letting them know about your book and that you think an interview with you would be a good fit for their audience. You can find some more tips on how to get interviewed here (www.radioguestlist.com/how-to-get-interviewed-on-podcasts-for-free-radio-publicity.html).

There are lots of things you can do - think outside the square and you'll realize there are plenty of opportunities to continue to increase your sales on Amazon.

In the final section of this book launch chapter, I'm going to provide you with my monthly marketing checklist. This is what I do to maintain all my book sales. But my number one strategy for keeping book sales going is to publish more books. So far, I have now published 5 books (including this one) in the space of 4 months!

Now I know that this is your side hustle, so you probably don't have as much time to dedicate to writing one book a month - that's ok, even if you only have 5 hours per week to write a book, you can still publish one book every two months. The key is to keep going and be consistent with your writing. The more you write, the faster you'll get and you'll find that writing a book a month, even as a side hustle, is actually achievable.

Ok, let's jump into the monthly marketing checklist. Turn the page to learn what I'm doing to keep my books selling at least 5 books per day!

Monthly Marketing Phase

OK, NOW we're getting into the meat of keeping you're side hustle income in the $1000 per month vicinity. Remember, you can't just publish your book and then forget about it, it takes some tending to keep it going.

The monthly checklist below only takes me about 30 minutes to execute for each book. Add it to your schedule and make it part of your monthly routine and you'll start to see ongoing traction with your books.

The Monthly Checklist

1. Review Keywords & Categories

It doesn't matter when you published your books (outside of the first 30 days of course), you need to be reviewing their keywords and categories to make sure that they are still ranking for those terms.

Let's start with keywords. Take each keyword and search with it on Amazon. In the search results, your book should be in the top 5. If it's not, then you'll want to find a better keyword to replace this one. Use MerchantWords, Google Keyword Planner and the Hot New Releases list to find better keywords.

Rinse and repeat for each keyword and then update your KDP area.

Once you've done this, review your categories. Is your book still in the Top 20 for each of it's categories? If it's not, then you need to change your categories.

You will likely switch between 4-6 different categories each month. This is why it's good to have a list of categories and cross-categories that your books can fit into.

The best way to do this is to view similar books in your categories and see where else these ones are ranking. Switch your book to any two categories as needed. Again, you'll update this in your KDP area.

2. Tweak Book Descriptions

Review your book descriptions every month as well, particularly if you have a fiction book. You'll want to update your description with any of the new keywords you've changed and where possible, look to include titles or subtitles from new books that are ranking well in your categories.

Be careful that you don't copy any other descriptions word for word. This will be seen as duplicate content and can affect your ratings, and if the original author happens to find out, you could find yourself being slapped with a ban from Amazon.

ALWAYS reword as much as possible. If you're ever unsure, use Copyscape.com to check to make sure you aren't creating duplicate content.

Again, you'll need to make changes in your KDP area.

3. Get More Reviews

Another way to maintain your sales and to keep your book in the top 20 in each of it's categories is to continue to push for reviews.

To do this, reach out to your networks, Facebook groups etc and remind people who have bought your book to leave a review. You could also drop your book to $0.99 for a few days to increase reviews as well.

If you have an email list, you could offer your book for free in exchange for a review.

Another option is to pay for verified reviews. Fiverr has many gigs where people will buy your book and provide you with an honest review. This can take some time and you are not guaranteed a 5-star review. It's a good strategy to keep review's happening though, so if you have the spare funds to do this, I would recommend it.

There are also websites that offer this service too. Here are a few to kick things off for you:

- Authors Cave
- The Kindle Book Review

- <u>The Indie Review</u>

4. Social Media Promotions/Links

As part of your monthly maintenance, you should also be sending traffic to your Amazon book page. Again, I'd recommend using Fiverr to do this. Only do one of the options below, any more than that and it's a waste of money.

- Link Pyramid
- Link Wheel
- Tweets
- Facebook shares
- Bookmarking Site submissions

When choosing your Fiverr gigs, make sure that they are high rating gigs and where possible, that they provide manual links for the link pyramid, wheels and bookmarking.

Now, if you're not familiar with what these all are, that's

ok, I'll explain how they work. For anyone familiar with SEO, you might be concerned with using link pyramids and wheel's, but I'll explain why you don't need to be too concerned.

Link Pyramid: this was one of the backlinking strategies that was first created to rank a website in search engines like Google. A link pyramid is made up of different tier's as follows - Tier 1: high authority links and high PR links, Tier 2: medium quality links and Tier 3: high quality links (but lots of them). Tier 1 links point directly to your Amazon book page (NOT your affiliate link), Tier 2 links point to Tier 1 and Tier 3 links point to Tier 2. They all link together in a pyramid shape.

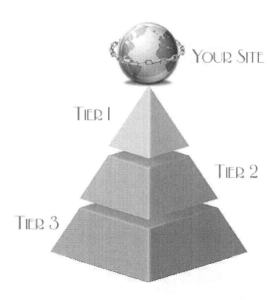

While this type of strategy can be seen as spam by Google for a 'normal' website, because you are linking to a high authority site like Amazon, this strategy does not hurt Amazon or your book.

When buying this type of gig on Fiverr, make sure that you only work with those that manually create the link pyramid. If you're unsure, always ask them for proof of previous work. They will provide you with a spreadsheet with all the manual links after your gig is complete.

Link Wheel: similar to a link pyramid, a link wheel is a collection of 5 or more web 2.0 properties (typically with a high page rank) that are then used to create backlinks to your Amazon book page. The wheel Is constructed by creating links between one unique web 2.0 property to another unique web 2.0 property and so on, while also pointing a backlink from each to your Amazon book page.

Again, this is to help a site rank in Google. After Google released their Penguin algorithm update, this affected a lot of sites that had this in place. Again, because Amazon has such a high ranking domain and is considered an authority site, a link wheel is not going to cause any issues. Again, if you do buy this gig on Fiverr, make sure that the link wheel is manually created.

Bookmarking Site Submission: this is a social bookmarking service that enables users to add, annotate, edit and share bookmarks of websites or documents. Delicious is a popular bookmarking site. Using this type of service the Fiverr gig would create a whole bunch of bookmarks that reference your books page on Amazon, utilizing tags (keywords) to create collections. This type of service is not frowned on by Google and is a great way to increase traffic to your site.

Social Media Promotions: this could be on Facebook, Twitter, Google+ or Pinterest. You are paying someone to share your book's page across their networks. If accessing this service on Fiverr, make sure that you only work with those gigs that have a high rating and provide you with proof of where they share your Facebook post or Tweet.

There you have it - my monthly marketing checklist. I recommend that you do 1-3 every month and choose one option from number 4 each month. And as I've already said, continuing to publish more books will also increase exposure to your already published books.

And that's the end of **Section 1 - You the eBook Writer!** In the next section, I'm going to show you how you can make money ghostwriting ebooks for other people.

On the next page, you'll find a Launch Plan so that you don't get lost along the way. The launch plan provides you with a timeline for each phase so that you know when to do what. Once you've published a few books, you can amend this to suit your own timelines. Turn the page to learn more.

Launch Plan

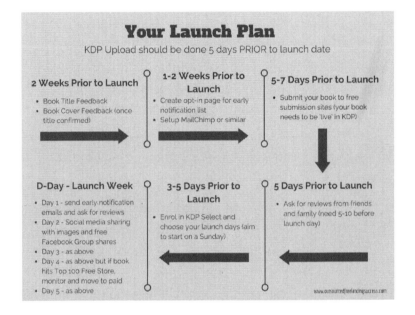

USE the launch plan as your go-to guide as you work your way through the process. Don't forget to schedule these days into your calendar once you've figured out your launch date.

On the next page you'll find the action checklist that covers even more of what you need to hit during the book launch phase. If you get stuck, just circle back or read the corresponding section. Turn the page to find out more.

Step 5 - Action List

REMEMBER, THESE checklists are here to ensure that you don't forget anything and that you follow the process. If you get stuck, circle back to the last step or back to the beginning and just start from scratch.

:: Checklist

- Upload your final book to KDP 5 days prior to your launch date
- Complete the steps outlined in the Pre-Launch Phase
- Enrol your book in KDP select and choose your free promotion dates (preferably start on a Sunday)
- Complete the steps outlined in the Launch Phase (this is launch week)
- Complete the steps outlined in the Post-Launch Phase
- Review the Monthly Marketing Checklist and complete those options you're happy to work with
- Review the Launch Plan and amend as needed

Now that we've gotten through the five steps (and action checklists), for self publishing a successful ebook, it's time to look at Section 2 - Ghostwriting eBooks. Turn the page to find out if this is something you're interested in doing!

Section 2 - You The Ghostwriter

What is Ghostwriting?

IF YOU'VE never heard of the term 'ghostwriting' before, here's a brief explanation so we're both on the same page for this section:

A ghostwriter is a 'writer for hire' who is paid to write an ebook, but takes none of the credit for the ebook once it's completed. This means that your name does not appear as an author for the book nor would it appear as a contributor. You are giving all rights to the work your write over to the person paying you to ghost write the ebook.

This might sound odd to you, but it's quite a common practice. Many people use ghostwriters, not just to write ebooks, but to write blog posts, speeches, social media posts etc. In fact, for many of my clients, I ghostwrite their social media posts. I act like I'm them - this is ghost writing at a simple level.

Ghostwriting is a lucrative area to get into, but it's important that you understand that if you decide to head down this track, you're still trading dollars for hours.

Ghostwriting ebooks is a great side hustle to do because it allows you to charge higher rates, get paid what you're worth for the writing you do but take on none of the responsibility (or recognition) associated with being the author of a book.

This is a great option if you're worried about anyone finding out that you're writing ebooks, as your name will never appear on any of the ebooks you ghost write, unless you negotiate that to happen.

As a ghost writer, you can charge higher rates because you're doing all the work. You can charge even more if you're an expert in a certain field, such as a doctor, nurse, vet etc.

You can also negotiate different deals with the author, depending on what you're writing. As an example, you could take a lower fee if the book you're writing is likely to sell widely and sell well. You could opt to take a $10,000 advance to write the book (we're talking large books here, in excess of 300 pages) which could be a lump sum or part payment. Then you could opt to take 10-20% of the books gross profits over a specified period of time or once it hit a ceiling cap that you'd agreed on. This type of deal would only work when the book is nearly guaranteed to be published for high profits. This would be a traditionally published book in most instances.

From a self-publishing viewpoint, you could take a lower

fee if you were listed as a contributor or editor of the book and would receive some of the gross profits. Similarly, if the book was less than 25,000 words, you might accept a lower payment.

There is a lot of competition in this space for cheap, quick ghost written books, but more often than not, these are low quality books. You want to find the clients that are prepared to pay you what you're worth and are looking for quality.

Finding Good Clients

To find good clients, review some of the sites below:

- Elance - this would be the place I'd start as there are a lot of people looking for ghost writers to write ebooks
- The Write Life - the job board on here provides some great opportunities for freelance writers
- Freelance Writing - great job board that curates a lot of freelance writing jobs including jobs for ghost writers
- Funds for Writers - a good site to find ghost writing ebook jobs

Once you've found a few options, submit your proposal and get yourself hired! If you're not sure what to include in your proposal, you'll find information about this on the

Resources Page. You will also find this information in the first Side Hustle Blueprint book - so refer to that if you have it (www.outsourcedfreelancingsuccess.com/ SideHustleBlueprint).

Now, you've got a client so you're ready to get started. Turn the page to start your ghostwriting side hustle the right way!

8. Step 1 - Project Details

Confirm Details

CONGRATULATIONS! A client has hired you to ghost write their ebook. Before you hit the ground running, you need to confirm a few things:

1. What keywords they are looking to rank for (this is relevant for both fiction or non-fiction)
2. What deadline they are looking to stick too
3. Contract and payment details

In most cases, the client will have already conducted the research and have a lot of information to provide to you. If they haven't done this and expect you to do this, make sure that you've incorporated that into your price point.

If you are having to do the research and find keywords, review **Section 1 - Chapters 3-4** to complete this stage.

1. Keywords
If the client has done the research, confirm with them what their keywords (if they haven't provided these to you already) are and then ask to be provided with all the information you'll need to get started.

If the client isn't sure what you mean when referring to keywords, ask them what categories they plan to place the book in once they publish it on Amazon. This will help you figure the keywords out and provide you with a bit more direction when you start writing the book.

2. Deadline

At this point, you should already be aware of the deadline, but it also pays to ask if the client wants you to provide them with work as it's completed. Some clients like to receive completed work as you progress through the book.

Make sure you also confirm how they wish to receive the work, i.e., in a MS word document, Google doc, text file etc.

Make sure you're clear on these two aspects and don't start any work until you are.

3. Contract & Payment

The final part of confirming your project details is making sure that you have a clear contract in place that outlines the above as well as when you'l be paid. If you're using a third party site like Elance, they take care of this for you and it's clear how you'll be paid and what the deadline is.

If you're not working with a site like Elance, make sure that you have something in writing that clearly outlines requirements and payment.

A service I use to ensure that everyone is on the same page is called www.ourdeal.com - they provide contracts for all situations that have been written by lawyers. You fill in the blanks and electronically send it to your client for digital signing. It then comes back to you for safe keeping.

I use this both as a contractor and contractee. It's handy to have a document to refer to if you're not sure of an aspect of the project and it also provides you with a degree of protection should something go wrong.

Once the above is clarified and you're sure of the project scope, it's time to start ghostwriting that ebook!

Turn the page to complete the checklist for this section. This will ensure that you don't miss a thing as you go through this process.

Step 1 - Action List

BELOW YOU'LL find a checklist to keep you on track as a ghostwriter. Check the points off and you're on your way to completing your first ghostwriting gig!

:: Checklist

- Confirm project details with the client
- Make sure they have provided keywords they are looking to rank for
- Make sure your deadline is clear and ask if and when completed work should be sent
- Ask the client how they would like the final document delivered
- Ensure that you have a contract in place that clearly outlines everything mentioned above as well as how much you'll be paid and when

Once you've checked everything off the list above, it's time to move onto the next chapter. Turn the page to get started as a ghostwriter!

9. Step 2 - Write the Book

Mind Map and Book Outline

BEFORE YOU start the ghostwriting process, you need to figure out what you're going to write first! It's not enough to have been provided with an outline from the client, you need to have an idea yourself about the topic you're writing about. You need a plan.

Here's the steps to take BEFORE you start to write.

Mind map the book idea

Rather than just jump straight into writing the book, it pays to provide yourself with a bit of a plan of how you're going to attack this process. I don't know about you, but I find it pretty difficult to just sit down and start writing without some sort of guide, especially if I want the writing to be good that is.

This is why, before you even start the writing process, you need to mind map the book idea. You should do this whether the book is fiction or non-fiction.

I know there are plenty of mind mapping tools available, but to be honest, I find that putting pen to paper 'releases' the flow of ideas more so than using an online tool or app. So I would recommend that you do this too.

I like to use a large piece of poster sized paper and write as much as I know about the topic. Use what the client has provided you as a basis and then look to come up with ideas yourself. This is particularly useful if you're ghostwriting a non-fiction book. If you're ghostwriting a fiction book, take the characters and plot line and expand your ideas from there.

I recommend you take a couple of hours to do this.

Outline the book
Once you've been through the mind mapping phase, you're now ready to outline the book further, organizing chapters and starting the ghostwriting process!

I like to us Evernote to outline my books and I also use it to capture research about each book.

Even though your client will have provided you with an outline, I find that writing the outline again, once I've mind mapped, provides me with a better sense of how I'm going to write the book and the information I might need to further research.

In the next section, we're going to look at ways that you can further research your topic, particularly if you're writing a non-fiction book. Turn the page to get started.

Researching 101

AS I mentioned in the project details chapter, you should have been provided with some information from the client with regards to research and keywords.

Even if you've been provided with a ton of research, it doesn't hurt to do a little yourself. And if you are tasked with doing the research, the following tips will help even more.

Keyword Research Tips
1. Use the keywords the client has provided to you and do simple Google searches and see what comes up. You're looking for information that is relevant to the topic and direction of the book. Once you find what you're looking for, use the 'web clipper' from Evernote to save it to your research notebook for this book.
2. Use your local library as well, particularly if you're looking for historical information.
3. Use Feedly to search for relevant news items on your topic. Buzz sumo is another great site to help you do this. Again, you'll need to use the keywords the client provided to do the searches.
4. Jump on YouTube and see if there are any relevant videos about the topic or keywords. Similarly, do the same on TEDx, particularly if you're

ghostwriting a non-fiction book.

5. Review the mind map you created and see if other information jumps off the page that you should research further.

Once you've got this information compiled together, go through and create a summary document for each article, blog post, news item, video etc. This will help some of the information 'stick' in your memory for you to recall when you start writing the book.

If you want to ensure that this information 'stick's' even more, only summarise documents as you go through each chapter that the document relates to.

If you start out summarizing the research first, then outline the chapter and then start the ghostwriting process, you'll find that information flows more freely than if you went through and summarized the research upfront.

It's also a good idea to mind map some of the items you read, particularly the video's, so you can capture high level ideas and use these further down the ghostwriting track.

Another few good resources, particularly from a non-fiction standpoint, are websites reddit.com and quora.com - both of these provide answers to questions that people ask. Maybe you can find some more information on these sites about the books topic.

If you're writing fiction, you'll need to do more fact checking research than anything. This is to ensure accuracy and so that you aren't portraying a location in the wrong way.

In the next section, we're going to look at your writing tool options. Turn the page to get started.

Choose a Writing Tool

IF THE client has provided you with how they want the document to be delivered (which they should have) you can choose to write straight into that end program, or you can use a tool like Scrivener (https://www.literatureandlatte.com/trial.php) and 'export' the document and save it in the format the client wants it.

Writing Tool Options

As I mentioned in the first section of this book, if you want to make a serious go at being an ebook writer, whether for yourself or as a ghostwriter, you need to learn how to use Scrivener.

Scrivener is the ONLY tool you should ever use to write with. Yes, you can use MS Word or Google Docs, but both of these will cause major headaches when you get further down the track and are ready to publish your own books.

As a ghostwriter, no matter what the end document needs to be, still do your writing in Scrivener, you'll find life so much easier. You can convert the document to a MS Word document or PDF, so there is no reason not to use Scrivener during the ghostwriting process.

The price for this tool is $40, but you can trial it for 30

actual days of use. What this means is that if you OPEN it every day for 30 days, that's your trial period. But if you only open it 2 days per week, your trial period will last for 15 weeks. So you can see how you can use this without having to pay for it initially.

If you want a quick crash course on how to use Scrivener, watch the video's on the Resources Page. Scrivener is a bit of a learning curve, but if you can dedicate the time (2-3 hours) to learn what you need to know, it will be your hero further down the track.

If you don't want to learn something new, I get it and I understand - go ahead and use MS Word or Google Docs.

Turn the page to complete the checklist for this section. This will ensure that you don't miss a thing as you go through this new process.

Step 2 - Action List

BELOW YOU'LL find a checklist to keep you on track as a ghostwriter. Check the points off and you're on your way to completing your first ghostwriting gig!

:: Checklist

- Mind map the initial book idea
- Outline the book in Evernote, even though the client has provided an outline for you
- Research the book using the ideas outlined (if required)
- Choose a writing tool
- Start writing! Refer to Chapter 4 in Section 1 for tips on mastering the Writing Mindset

In the next section, we're going to look at the editing process. This process is slightly different compared with if you're writing an ebook as the author. Turn the page to get started.

10. Step 3 - Editing

Self Editing

CONGRATULATIONS! YOU'VE written your first ghostwritten ebook and you're now ready to edit the book before you hand it to the client...

The self-editing phase is done in three parts, initial read through, read out loud then run through using the Hemingway app. You need to make sure that you complete this phase thoroughly before handing it back to the client.

If you're providing the client with completed work as you work your way through the ebook, you'll need to ensure that you complete the self-editing phase on each piece of content prior to handing it over to the client.

Phase 1 – Read Through

Allow yourself a few hours to complete this. If you're using Scrivener, as I like to do, then turn on 'Revision Mode' choosing the 'first revision' option, which is a nice red for easy identification.

You will find Revision Mode located under 'Format' in the top menu drop down box. Once turned on, it's applied to your entire document. You can tell that it's on in two ways:

1.   When you type, the words are in red, and
2.   The text color option displays as red

During the read through, I find that I tend to get rid of quite a bit of fluff – sentences and paragraphs that don't add to the book in any way. You should aim to do the same.

I also look for filler words, words that don't add to the meaning of a sentence or phrase. For example, when you're ghostwriting a first draft, you'll probably find that you overuse the words "very" and "the" a lot! By removing them, you instantly improve the quality of your writing and the book by a good 30-40 percent.

Follow these quick tips when self-editing:

1.   Remove fluff content – anything that isn't important or required to get the point across
2.   Remove filler words – words like "very' and "the" as examples
3.   Add stories to help illustrate your points where needed

This last point is important. If you're writing non-fiction, you need to be able to connect with the client's audience. Telling stories helps to do this and also illustrates your points further. Of course, if you're writing a fiction book, this goes without saying, you're telling stories left, right and centre!

If you're writing a fiction book, a lot of this doesn't apply. When you do your initial read through, you'll be looking for grammar issues or spelling errors mainly.

Phase 2- Read Out Loud

One of the easiest ways to identify 'fluff' is to read through your book from cover to cover, but read it out loud. If you stumble over any words or phrases, then these are the ones you'll want to remove or reword. Do this type of editing immediately after your initial read through above.

Once you've complete these two phases, you need to run it through an app that I love, particularly from a non-fiction writing point of view.

Phase 3 - Hemingway App

This app (www.hemingwayapp.com/) will tell you if your grammar is crap, will identify spelling errors , sentence difficulty from a reading point of view plus so much more. It will force you to simplify your sentences, depending on who the target audience is.

It works for both fiction and non-fiction books. You can use it for free on the web, or your can get the pro version for

$6.99 which allows you to download the desktop app. Choose what works for you.

A word of caution: as you go through the app, if something doesn't feel right to you, don't change it. Your client will let you know if it works or not. The Hemingway App is a great way to tidy up your work before you unleash it on the client!

Once you've completed the self-editing phase, you're ready to finish the book and hand it over to the client for feedback and fix any minor changes.

Turn the page to complete the checklist for this section. This will ensure that you don't miss a thing as you go through the self-editing process.

Step 3 - Action List

BELOW YOU'LL find a checklist to keep you on track as a ghostwriter. Check the points off and you're on your way to completing your first ghostwriting gig!

:: Checklist

- Complete a thorough read through of the text
- Read the book out loud so you can pick up any sentences or words that cause you to stumble as your read
- Run all of your text through the Hemingway App to make sure it flows correctly and that you haven't missed any grammar or spelling issues

In the next section, we're going to look at finalizing the book. It's time to get the book ready to hand over to the client and get their feedback. Turn the page to get started.

11. Step 4 - Finish Book

Completion of eBook Project

WELL DONE you! You're almost done. How are you feeling about the ghostwriting process, now that you've been through the majority of it?

It's important to note at this point that ghostwriting isn't for everyone. If you are interested in turning this side hustle into a full-time gig, writing your own ebooks is the better way to go. You'll make more money in the long-run as you'll be able to build your own email list and author platform.

As a ghostwriter, you're unable to do this effectively because you're still trading hours for dollars. Don't get me wrong, ghostwriting is still a great side hustle, especially if you're just looking to make a bit of side income and don't have any desire to leave your job anytime soon.

Now that you've completed the self-editing process, there are just a couple of things you should do before you hand the finished product back to the client.

Finishing the eBook

1. Review the book against the project details and the clients original outline - do they gel? Does the book follow what the client originally wanted you to do? If it doesn't, then you'll need to go back through and make any necessary changes.

2. Have you added intro and outro sections to each chapter? An intro covers (briefly) what the previous chapter covered and the outro summarizes what the reader has just learned and what's coming up next. This applies mainly to non-fiction books, but can be utilized in fiction books - it's best to check with your client first if you're writing a fiction book about adding this aspect.

3. If possible and time permits, have your partner or a close friend read through the book so that you've got a second pair of eyes to view the content for you.

4. Make sure you convert the file to the correct format as per the clients request. If you used Scrivener, you can compile to a variety of options.

Once you're happy with the final product, submit it to the client!

Depending on your relationship with the client and your skill base, now would be a good opportunity to let them know about your other services.

These might include:

- Book marketing (if you want to know more about how this works, refer back to **Section 1 - Chapter 7 - Book Launch**
- Content writing - obviously the client now knows you can write, so if you wanted to offer this as an ongoing service, now is the time to highlight this to them

If you're happy to just keep your side hustle simple, stick with ghostwriting only.

Once you've been ghostwriting for a while, be sure to refer to Section 1 of this book and decide whether you could make it as a self-published ebook writer instead. The satisfaction you get out of publishing your own work is incomparable, in my humble opinion.

12. What's Next

Where to From Here?

"HAVE FAITH in yourself. Think yes, not no. Live life to the full. NEVER give up." ~ Richard Branson

Let's do a quick recap on what we've covered:

- ✓ You learned how to be an ebook writer and self-publish your own book on Amazon
- ✓ We covered how to launch your book properly and how to maintain the sales of that book
- ✓ You learned how to make money as a ghostwriter of ebooks rather than an author
- ✓ We covered how to ensure that you get the right information from the client about the project
- ✓ You learned how to ghostwrite the ebook and how to edit it
- ✓ Lastly, we covered how to properly complete your project and deliver it to the client

Does that about cover everything? It's a lot of stuff to cover in one sitting, so make sure you have understood each chapter before you move onto each step through the two different sections.

Review the checklists at the end of each chapter, they

cover everything you need to do to get yourself up and running as either an eBook Writer or Ghostwriter of eBooks.

Use them to follow along and check your progress with setting up your side hustle and to ensure you don't miss a key step along the way.

Review everything on the resources page and if you get stuck, double back and follow the steps. And if you really can't move forward, send me an email - lise@outsourcedfreelancingsuccess.com.

Follow a Plan

EARNING AN extra $1000 in 30 days is achievable, if you take action. If you don't take action, nothing will change and you definitely won't be in the green by $1000.

Remember, **Learn, Do, Repeat**. That's what successful author's do - let's add your name to that list!

Congratulations! You're now equipped to start making some money from your eBook Writing or Ghostwriting eBooks side hustle.

Complete the action steps at the end of each chapter, follow the writing and launch plans, use the checklists to make sure you've got everything set up and get your writing side hustle making you some money.

Do all this and you could be kissing your normal job good-bye in a short 8-10 months like I did!

If you have any questions or would like to provide some feedback, I'd welcome an email from you. Just send it to lise@outsourcedfreelancingsuccess.com and I'll respond within 24 hours.

Now don't just sit there, follow the steps, print the documents found on the Resources Page, take action and

I'll see you on the other side!

Remember, do what you love...

"The struggle you're in today is developing the strength you need for tomorrow." ~ www.dailyquotes.co

Acknowledgements

There were so many people that inspired me to write this book, and there were also so many amazing people that helped refine my ideas and make this book come to life. Thank you for your support and for helping to make this book great!

I'd like to give a big shout out to Chandler and James for all your support with my self-publishing career. You guys provide so much inspiration, I'm eternally grateful to have 'met' you both!

About the Author

Lise is an author, blogger and sometimes-social media consultant and a self-confessed shoe fanatic – she's obsessed. Just ask her husband!

She has been looking for the magic in life since she was first exposed to positive, happy thoughts at the tender age of one - thanks Mum and Dad!

Lise can regularly be found at local cafes, NOT drinking coffee, but the more sophisticated and magical beverage that is a *Chai Latte*. She's also a bit of a baller, building her self-publishing empire an a crazy rate (think 3 books in 2 months!).

Her online home is located at
OutsourcedFreelancingSuccess.com.

Can you help?

Can you help? If you liked this book and it was helpful to you, could you please leave a review on Amazon? Simply swipe (turn the page) to leave your review!

As a huge THANK YOU for doing this, <u>send me an email</u> with a link to your VERIFIED review and you'll get **30 minutes with me on a Skype call** - you can ask me any burning questions you have about **starting your eBook Writing or Ghostwriting Side Hustle!**

Other Books by Lise Cartwright

No Gym Needed Series
- No Gym Needed: Quick & Simple Workouts for Gals on the Go
- No Gym Needed: Quick & Simple Workouts for Busy Guys

If you're not a fan of the gym and like to get your exercise done in 30 minutes or less - these books are right up your alley!

Side Hustle Series
- Book 1: Side Hustle Blueprint: How to Make an Extra $1000 per month Without Leaving Your Day Job
- Book 2: You're reading it!

oDesk Guides
- The Definitive Guide to Getting Freelance Writing Work on oDesk
- How to Pimp Your oDesk Profile

And if you want access to more books like this, sign up for the Lise's **New Releases** mailing list to get access to early notification of new book releases, discounts and freebies!

Click here to get started: www.lisecartwright.com

Wealth Transformation Journal

Made in the USA
San Bernardino, CA
03 January 2015